QUICK GUIDE TO
INTERACTION STYLES

AND WORKING REMOTELY 2.0

Strategies for
Leading and Working
in Virtual Teams

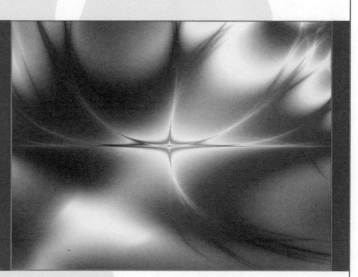

SUSAN K. GERKE
LINDA V. BERENS

Telos

PUBLICATIONS

Published By:
Telos Publications
P.O. Box 4457, Huntington Beach, California 92605-4457
http://www.telospublications.com

International Standard Book Number: 978-0-9844220-0-5

Cover Image: Split Ends
©2001 Damien Jones. Used with permission.
Cover/Layout Design/Illustrations: Kris Kiler Marketing Design
Illustrations: Chris Berens of Thumbnail Productions

Ordering Information

Individual Sales U.S.: This publication can be purchased directly from the Telos Publications Web site or at the address above.

Individual Sales International: A list of international distributors can be received directly from the Telos Publications Web site or at the address above.

Quantity Sales: Special discounts are available on quantity purchases by corporations, associations, and others. Details can be received at the Telos Publications Web site or at the address above.

Orders for College Textbook/Course Adoption Use: Information can be received directly from the Telos Publications Web site or at the address above.

Orders by U.S./International Trade Bookstores and Wholesalers: Information can be received directly from the Telos Publications Web site or at the address above.

Training is available for further exploration of the information provided in this book.

> Contact:
> Interstrength® Associates
> http://www.interstrength.com

Interstrength® Associates, formerly Temperament Research Institute (TRI), is a training and consulting company dedicated to serving individuals and organizations seeking to improve their overall functioning through more accurate self-knowledge, knowledge of others, effective communication, and teamwork.

This book is dedicated to
• Dave Gerke for his unwavering support.
• John Berens for his wonderful Behind-the-Scenes support and trust.

Acknowledgments
• All the individuals who read descriptions and gave us feedback.
• The many students in workshops over the years who have shared their challenges and solutions for working remotely.
• Scott Campbell, Linda Ernst, Judy Gareis, Julie Mallory, and Melissa Smith for their enthusiastic embrace of the Interaction Styles model and for putting it to work in their own practices.
• Kris Kiler for encouraging us to write this book.

About the Authors

Susan K. Gerke, B.S.

Susan K. Gerke is the president of Gerke Consulting & Development and "helps people work better, together." Susan's focus since 1989 has been in designing, customizing and implementing leadership and teamwork programs meeting the needs of executives, managers, and employees in a wide number of companies and industries. A recognized expert on remote leadership and teaming, Susan has applied her skill and knowledge in facilitation, curriculum development and coaching. Susan's expertise comes from many years of being a remote worker herself as well as a leader of people at a distance. Thousands of remote leaders and workers have increased their effectiveness in their remote environments as a result of attending Susan's workshops. Susan uses the Interaction Styles model extensively in her work and is a faculty member of Interstrength® Associates.

Other titles by Susan K. Gerke:

- *The I in TEAM* (2005)
- *Quick Guide to the Interaction Styles and Time Dynamics* (2007)

Linda V. Berens, Ph.D.

Linda V. Berens is the director and founder of Interstrength® Associates, which provides organizational consulting and interventions as well as certiication in the Interstrength Method. She has qualified hundreds of professionals to administer and interpret the Myers-Briggs Type Indicator® (MBTI®) instrument. She is an organizational consultant and has spent over thirty-four years helping individuals and teams recognize their strengths, transcend their weaknesses, and work together better. Her organizational consulting centers on helping whole organizations release hidden potential. Linda is recognized internationally for her theoretical contributions to the field of psychological type and for developing user-friendly training materials for practical application of understanding individual differences. Linda has both worked remotely and managed faculty and associates remotely for many years.

Other titles by Linda V. Berens:

- *The 16 Personality Types: Descriptions for Self-Discovery* (1999)
- *Understanding Yourself and Others®: An Introduction to the 4 Temperaments—4.0* (2010)
- *Understanding Yourself and Others®: An Introduction to Interaction Styles 2.0* (2009)
- *Understanding Yourself and Others®: An Introduction to the Personality Type Code* (2003)
- *Understanding Yourself and Others®: The 16 Personality Types: Descriptions for Self-Discovery* (1999)
- *Working Together: A Personality-Centered Approach to Management* (1995)
- *Quick Guide to the16 Personality Types and Teams* (2004)
- *The I in TEAM* (2005)

Contents

Note pad

Leading and Teaming

The workplace has changed. We can no longer assume that the people we need to work with will be in our same location, let alone the same time zone. These people include our managers, peers, teammates, and direct reports. When we are not in the same location or working in the same time zone, we are working remotely.

This booklet is designed with two purposes in mind. The first is to help you understand the issues associated with working remotely. The second is to provide techniques for being successful when working remotely.

Some of you are in leadership roles and some are not. Some of you work on teams and some do not. We have put emphasis in three areas: leading, teaming, and individual contributor.

What Is Leading?

When we talk about leading, we are talking about the role you play when you are responsible for someone else's output. This could be a manager, a project manager, a team leader, or some other type of leader particular to your organization.

Leading can include a number of activities such as setting goals, providing feedback, assigning tasks or projects, managing projects, and so on.

What Is Remote Leading?

Remote leading occurs when the person who is leading works in a different location (country, city, building, floor) or at a different time (shift, time zone) from one or more followers. When the leader or a follower travels extensively, the relationship between the two may be a remote relationship even though they may have desks in the same location. What often defines the relationship as remote is whether there is a need to schedule time to meet versus counting on casual opportunities for interacting.

What Is Teaming?

Teaming describes the activities two or more people engage in to do work together. They may be on a formal work team or project team, or they may just have the need to accomplish something together.

Generally when people are teaming, they have a common goal or objective as well as an interdependence on each other to accomplish the work. They may be teaming on just a portion of their jobs, but that portion requires them to interact.

What Is Remote Teaming?

Remote teaming occurs when two or more employees are working together on a common work product, problem, or task and one or more of them is working in a different location (country, city, building, floor) or at a different time (shift, time zone).

What Is an Individual Contributor?

Any employee who is not part of a team is an individual contributor. Some employees participate in teams sometimes and work as individual contributors the rest of the time.

What Is a Remote Individual Contributor?

A remote individual contributor is an employee who works in a different location (country, city, building, floor) or at a different time (shift, time zone) from his or her manager.

How Remote Is Remote?

Remoteness can have degrees. We can describe four common points on a continuum of remoteness relative to location.

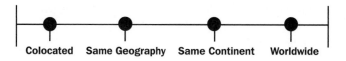

Colocated   Same Geography   Same Continent   Worldwide

- Colocated—not remote
- Same city/general geography—can get together on occasion (drive/walk)
- Same continent—can meet less often (fly)
- Worldwide—may never meet face to face

We also can look at the degrees of remoteness relative to time. This also could be represented by a continuum with four points.

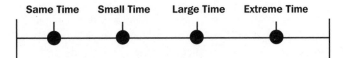

| Same Time | Small Time | Large Time | Extreme Time |

- Same time—We are both at work at the same time all the time (same time zone)
- Small time—We are both at work at the same time some of the time (small time zone differences, windows of opportunity to connect)
- Large time—We are never at work at the same time (different shifts or large time zone difference)
- Extreme time—We are never at work at the same time (extreme time zone difference and probably different days)

Why Talk about Working Remotely?

Is the need to work remotely just a passing phase? Before we decide yes or no, let's look at some of the key factors driving distance leadership.

First of all, many organizations today are merging or being acquired. When the companies are in different cities (for example, San Diego and Chicago), it is usually more cost effective to leave employees in each location. Over time, reorganization puts people in the two locations in the same work groups, and the need to work remotely emerges.

Another driver of remote work can be customers. If your customers demand that you have sales and/or support people located near them, you again will find yourself with people working remotely in order to remain competitive.

The growing reluctance of employees to relocate also is a driver of the increase in remote relationships. In a two-career family, it may be difficult for both workers to move. Responsibility for aging parents, commitments to the community, reluctance to have children change schools, and so on, can all influence employees to not want to relocate.

When an employee has critical skills and tacit company knowledge, companies are often more inclined to respond to some of his or her needs, such as working in a different city or working at home. Rather than lose the employee, companies are more willing to set up a remote relationship.

From an economic perspective, relocating people is very expensive for companies. Many companies are also finding they can save money on real estate by having people work from home.

What driving factors have caused your organization to have remote workers?

In addition to driving factors, a number of enablers have resulted in more remote working over the past few years. Technology is a key enabler. The advent and availability of cell phones, laptops, fast phone lines, portable data assistant's, conference calls, video conferences, and collaborative software have made it easy for people to connect from just about anywhere. And the technology just keeps getting better and cheaper, making it easier all the time to work remotely.

Another enabler of remote work is the movement of our society to an information society. Much of what workers need in order to do their jobs is available in company databases or on the Internet. No longer do we have to go to file cabinets in a central location to find the information we need.

In light of these key drivers and enablers, we think you will agree that working remotely is not just a fad or passing phase. If anything, we are likely to see more of it since it provides some real advantages, such as:

- Time to refine written communications so they can be well thought out and complete
- 24 hours a day that projects can be worked on as they are passed around the world
- Improved lifestyles for individuals
- Organizational flexibility
- The opportunity to bring together the best resources to do work

> *"95 percent of Fortune 1000 companies have implemented virtual work."*
> **—Trina Hoefling**

2

What Are the Issues for Leaders of Remote Employees/Teams?

Since working remotely is a fact of life, it is worth understanding the issues that tend to come along with working remotely.

Remote leaders tend to struggle with the following issues:

- Measuring performance when you are unable to see employees working
- Making sure everyone gets the same information or messages (this can refer to organizational information or any common information)
- Building trust
- Balancing workload among team members
- Getting to know employees on a more personal level
- Managing the additional travel required to meet face to face
- Understanding the issues the employees/teams have at their locations
- Knowing about conflict before it gets out of hand
- Identifying the need for developmental feedback
- Giving developmental feedback
- Spotting talent in your individual contributors
- Communicating without nonverbal cues (nearly 40 percent of a message is communicated via body language)

Are There Some Situations Where there Are Other Issues?

When the leader is not colocated with any team members, these may be issues:

- Pressures from others in the leader's location (often the leader's boss or peers)
- Additional staff work
- Feeling of isolation from the team and its issues

When the leader is colocated with some of the team but not others, these may be issues:

- Jealousy among team members
- Tendency to give work to those colocated
- Forgetting to communicate information with those not colocated
- Integration of new members into the team

When every member of the team is in a separate location (this is often true with people working at home, with sales organizations, or with people on cross-functional teams), these may be issues:

- Provision of mentoring or development opportunities
- Provision of visibility for team members
- Isolation of members
- More travel for the leader

> **As a remote leader, which of these issues do you find are challenging to you?**
>
> **What additional issues do you have as a remote leader?**

What Are the Issues for Individual Contributors?

Employees who are remote from their manager or peers tend to have some of the following issues:

- Locating your manager when you need him or her
- Feeling your manager does not know what you do
- Thinking your manager may be unaware when you are overloaded with work
- Understanding your company's business direction
- Having limited social interaction
- Lacking visibility in the organization
- Getting development opportunities (including being mentored)
- Not getting enough recognition
- Being pulled by others at your location to do work outside of your responsibilities (you may have a relationship with them)
- Getting incomplete communication (nonverbal cues missing)
- Having limited opportunities for casual relationship building
- Feeling disconnected or lonely
- Dealing with challenges of working at home (see Appendix B)

3

What Are the Issues for Teams?

In addition to the above issues, which affect individual team members, when teaming the following tend also to be issues:

- Building teamwork
- Building trust
- Knowing each other's skills
- Knowing each other's styles
- Resolving conflict
- Trusting each member to work independently
- Skillfully using multiple communication vehicles (fax, e-mail, voice mail, collaborative software, conference calling, etc.)

As an individual contributor or team member, which issues do you face?

What additional issues are challenging you?

We can more readily understand where some of these issues come from by looking at a map of the kinds of communication we can have. The Johari Window*, originally used for improving communication, is a useful map to help us understand some of the difficulties of working remotely.

The Johari Window*

	Known to Self	Unknown to Self
Known to Others	**Public Knowledge . . .** *What I Show You*	**Feedback . . .** *Your Gift to Me*
Unknown to Others	**Private . . .** *Mine to Share*	**Unconscious . . .** *Not to Probe, but I Can Become More Aware and Choose to Share*

For example, there is "Public Knowledge"— aspects we know about ourselves and that are known to others around us. These public aspects of ourselves are easily recognized when we are colocated with teammates. What do we talk about over coffee or around the water cooler? Our coworkers listen to what we say and how we say it. Opportunities for casually gaining this shared public knowledge abound when we are in the same physical space but are scarce when we are working remotely.

In the "Feedback" area of the Johari Window, we see that often people have information that we are unaware of. In a remote situation, giving and receiving this feedback is often more difficult to do, and thus our relationships may suffer unless we learn some tools for doing it. In the "Private" space of communications, we need to feel a sense of trust in order to self-disclose information that will make working remotely go more smoothly. And the "Unconscious" aspects of our selves need to be made more visible by having a language to talk about some of the differences that are more easily dealt with in person than they are remotely.

Because many of the issues that surface when working remotely have to do with relating to others, influencing others, and communicating, we have found that understanding a model of Interaction Styles can be extremely helpful in being effective. We'll introduce the model here and then integrate it into the solutions we present later.

> *"You never really understand a person until you consider things from his point of view."*
> **—Harper Lee**

---

*Originally formulated by Joseph Luft and Harry Ingham in "The Johari Window: A Graphic Model of Awareness in Interpersonal Relations," in *Group Process: An Introduction to Group Dynamics*, Joseph Luft (Palo Alto, Calif.: National Press Books, 1963), 10–12.

4

How We Do What We Do

The Interaction Style model addresses our styles of interacting with others—how we try to influence them and relate to them. It often determines whether we listen to someone or not and whether we like someone.

Interaction Style Patterns

Throughout the ages, observers of human behavior have repeatedly identified patterns or configurations of behavior. Such holistic sorting of behavior patterns has been recorded for at least twenty-five centuries.

All of these models suggest that these styles or types are inborn. In the meantime, studies continue to be conducted on the various "temperamental" traits that can be identified and tracked over time with physiological measures. Many of these traits seem to relate to the Interaction Style patterns. How do you find out which pattern fits you? There are several methods.

Self-Discovery*

One powerful way to find your best-fit Interaction Style pattern is through self-discovery. In this ongoing process, you learn about the four patterns while reflecting on which is most like you. This works very well for many people. (For more information about finding your natural Interaction Style, see *Understanding Yourself and Others: An Introduction to Interaction Styles* by Linda Berens.)

Self-Reflection

Self-reflection happens when we pay attention to what our behavior is and then compare that behavior to the descriptions of the different Interaction Styles. Since we will be looking at behavior, it is important to be aware that your public self may reflect adaptive or learned behavior. This adaptive self is also part of who you are but may not hold the key to what energizes you.

Interaction with Others

We also learn who we are through our interactions with others. Finding people who are similar to us and comparing notes and sharing stories helps many of us find our own best-fit Interaction Style pattern. This process often happens in workshops when people openly discuss their interaction styles in order to better understand themselves and others. Sometimes this kind of discussion takes us into the "Private" area of the Johari Window—those aspects known to ourselves and not known to others. In the same way, self-discovery often sends us to this area, at least privately.

One valuable way of finding out who we are is by actively seeking feedback—asking others to tell us how they see us. These people may be trained facilitators or merely people who know us well. The "Feedback" area of the Johari Window gives us the opportunity to learn about those aspects of ourselves unknown to us but known to others. This provides additional information as we explore who we are. And remember, this feedback is a gift, often given through the perspective of the giver. So as you seek to find a good fit with one of the Interaction Style patterns, ask many others for feedback.

Openness to New Information

During the self-discovery process, we sometimes have "Unconscious" information come into our minds— aspects previously unknown to ourselves and unknown to others. In the Interaction Style model, the unconscious is often where we "store" information about how to "be" in the world. As you explore who you are, stay open to valuable insights from this area.

Many variables may affect your self-discovery process. Be aware that family, social, cultural, and other influences will affect how you view yourself in relation to the Interaction Style patterns. These influences are often unconscious until they somehow come into our awareness when they are described and pointed out. Stay open and searching. Seek input from all areas of the Johari Window.

5

---

*Adapted, with permission, from Berens, Linda V., *Understanding Yourself and Others®: An Introduction to Interaction Styles* (Huntington Beach, Calif.: Telos Publications 2001).

Key Elements

Interaction Style Is Inborn

From an individual's earliest moments of existence, Interaction Style patterns can be observed in that person over and over again. These tendencies have been studied and tracked in many individuals over the course of their lifetimes.

Interaction Style Remains Constant

Our pattern of organization exists from the beginning and influences our growth and development. Our Interaction Style is expressed throughout our life. It is not merely a result of acquiring individual traits from our experiences. Rather, it is a constant internal drive to interact with others in certain ways.

Interaction Style Drives Behavior

Our behaviors cluster into activity patterns. These activity patterns organize around themes of drives, aims, core beliefs, and fears specific to each Interaction Style. When situations require us to adapt to environments and use behaviors inconsistent with our fundamental nature, our Interaction Style influences that adaptation as well.

Interaction Style Is Dynamic, Not Static; Influencing, Not Limiting

Interaction Style is a dynamic pattern, always open to influence from the environment. We come into the world with a predisposition, our core self, but growth does not stop with the predisposition. We are free to behave and develop in other ways. We can and do behave in situations in a variety of ways; this is our contextual self.

Consider roles, for example. Our Interaction Style pattern will influence which roles we are drawn to take with others and which ones we fulfill more easily. However, we can and do take roles that are characteristic of any Interaction Style in a given situation, and over time they become an aspect of our developed self.

Neither the developed self nor the core self determines what to do in a given situation. That is the role of our contextual self—to act according to the needs of the moment, choosing whether or not to be responsive to the influences of the core self and developed self.

Interaction Style Is a Pattern

Even though some of the evidence for the existence of the Interaction Style patterns comes from measurement of physiological traits, Interaction Style is best viewed as a whole pattern, not a cluster of traits. The pattern derives from neurophysiological tendencies.

Regardless of your best-fit Interaction Style pattern, you are likely to display some of the characteristics of other styles. On the whole, you are likely to find more of the descriptors of one style pattern than another fitting you. Those characteristics that do fit will more likely occur in response to a specific context rather than being the energy pattern that has been constant over your lifetime. For example, all people want to get a good result, yet only one Interaction Style has "getting the best result possible" as a driving force. People frequently choose ways of interacting that fit the overall pattern of their natural organization.

Interaction Style Is Organic

We seem to have a motoric predisposition to react to stimuli in certain ways. For example, some people respond quite actively and others respond in a more relaxed manner. These predispositions give us a tendency to take different stances in relation to others.

Interaction Style Is a Communication

These stances influence our points of view in any given situation. Our Interaction Style becomes a communication in and of itself. Communication theorists point out that all behavior is communication. In fact, it is impossible to not communicate. Even silence sends a message. The meaning of that message is interpreted through the lenses of the receiver who observes various postures and facial expressions. Thus, Interaction Style is an important aspect of communication that involves influencing others.

To find your Interaction Style, read the four brief descriptions and narrow your selection to two that are like you. Then as you read through the various advantages and disadvantages of each style, reflect on your experiences when working remotely and see which pattern speaks to you. You may find yourself relating to more than one pattern since you have likely adapted to a variety of situations and had to use styles that are different from your own. The most important application of Interaction Style differences in working remotely is gaining insight into why people behave differently from you. This understanding can keep you from misreading others' behavior as noncooperative or lacking interest. Use the hints offered in this book to make your communications and your work more effective.

Remember, each style has its own strengths and weaknesses for working remotely. And working remotely gives advantages to some styles and disadvantages to others.

Chart-the-Course

- Have a course of action in mind beforehand.
- Create a plan (or several workable plans).
- Keep the group on track, allowing for digressions as long as progress is being made.
- Devise, define, describe, or reveal the way to achieve the vision.
- Make deliberate decisions, checking against an already-thought-out process.
- Focus on giving guidance and illumination so the right decision is made.
- Analyze and figure out what needs to be done.
- Plan agendas for project completion and meetings.
- Conceptualize a desired result and how to get there.
- Foresee how people will respond and plan accordingly.

Behind-the-Scenes

- Do what it takes to get the best result possible.
- See value in contributions from many people or information sources.
- Support the group's process by allowing for digressions then refocusing on the desired outcome.
- Reconcile many voices in communication of the vision.
- Make consultative decisions, integrating many sources of input.
- Focus on understanding the process to get a high quality outcome.
- Aim to produce the best products and results.
- Support others as they do their work.
- Define specifications to meet standards and apply principles.
- Clarify values and intentions.

In-Charge

- Get things accomplished (often through people).
- Take rapid action to get things done and move on to the next project.
- Lead the group to the goal.
- Articulate the vision and create an environment to achieve it.
- Make quick decisions with confidence in what is needed.
- Focus on getting desired results as soon as possible.
- Execute actions, work all the angles, and remove obstacles.
- Supervise others and provide resources.
- Marshal and mobilize people, financial, and material resources.
- Mentor people, finding the talent and nurturing the talent to get the job done.

Get-Things-Going

- Get everyone involved participating.
- Move the group members to action along their paths.
- Facilitate the group's process to work with people where they are to get them to where they are going.
- Get the energy moving toward an emerging vision.
- Make enthusiastic, collaborative decisions that ensure buy-in.
- Focus on interactions to get more from the group than group members can get individually.
- Explore options that keep things moving along.
- Make preparations to make things easy for others.
- Discover new ways of seeing things and doing things.
- Share insights about what something means and what is really going on.

7

*Taken from Berens, Linda V., *Understanding Yourself and Others®: An Introduction to Interaction Styles* (Huntington Beach, Calif.: Telos Publications, 2001).

The theme of this style is getting things accomplished through people. People of this style are focused on results, often taking action quickly. They often have a driving energy with an intention to lead a group to the goal. They make decisions quickly to keep themselves and others on task, on target, and on time. They hate wasting time and having to backtrack. Mentoring, executing actions, supervising, and mobilizing resources are all ways they get things accomplished. They notice right away what is not working in a situation and become painfully aware of what needs to be fixed, healed, or corrected.

Strengths

The remote environment lets people of this style accomplish work at their own fast pace in situations where others are not involved. Their drive to accomplish and get things done may override some of the issues and obstacles others experience when working remotely. These remote challenges are experienced as nuisances rather than show-stoppers. They will tend to keep the group on task in conference calls and work to keep videoconferences on track. They adapt quickly to new tools when they see how the tools will help get the work accomplished.

Advantage of Working Remotely

Their nonverbal cues of impatience, which can sometimes shut down contributions of others, will not be as visible in the remote environment.

Challenges for Working Remotely

When working remotely, it can feel like the situation is out of control when someone of an In-Charge style is dependent on others and can't see work getting done. People of this style can also feel frustrated when they aren't involved in casual conversations where they can jump in with answers as they are naturally prone to do.

Potential Pitfalls

They may go ahead and make decisions for the good of the group or project without all the information they would have if they were colocated. This push to get things done quickly may also preclude the extra time it takes to get the involvement of others. On the phone, their impatience may be picked up through their intonation, clipped speech, sighs, and other cues.

Opportunity for Growth

If this is your style:

- Remember that some things may take longer in this environment—be patient.
- Be aware of how your voice is coming across on the telephone.
- Pause and listen.

Please Understand Them

People of this style would rather work face to face most of the time. They may prefer working remotely from someone whose style of working irritates them. They tend to get over conflicts and flareups quickly, and others may not be able to know that since they do not have the nonverbal cues to go by. People of this style need to know the end results, that the work will be finished on time and be of good quality. They want credit for their contributions.

Support Them

To support people of this style:

- Give the reason for taking longer or revisiting a topic.
- Give them feedback that you know they know what they are doing.
- Communicate what you will do and by when and then follow through on the commitment.
- Give main points, not details, unless asked.
- Be straightforward and ask for exactly what you want.
- Reassure them that progress is being made.
- Acknowledge them when you use their suggestions.

8

 The theme of this style is having a course of action to follow. People of this style focus on knowing what to do and keeping themselves, the group, or the project on track. They prefer to enter a situation having an idea of what is to happen. They identify a process to accomplish a goal and have a somewhat contained tension as they work to create and monitor a plan. The aim is not the plan itself but to use it as a guide to move things along toward the goal. Their informed and deliberate decisions are based on analyzing, outlining, conceptualizing, or foreseeing what needs to be done.

Strengths

The independence of working remotely is natural for people of this style. Their natural planfulness is an asset in this environment. They like time and space away from interaction and electronic tools that allow them to give thought to what to do. E-mail suits their desire to have a choice of response time and work with the content at a comfortable pace. For conference calls, they like to think things through ahead of time and create an agenda. They look forward to disengaging to get their work done.

Advantage of Working Remotely

Others often misread the detachment of this style as disinterest. People of this style are saved from having others misread their detachment by working remotely. Since they are outside the group space, others will not know they are not expressing a response.

Challenges for Working Remotely

Working remotely makes it easier to step back. As such, it may be harder for people of this style to become integrated members of the team. Long conference calls with pressure to make decisions and no tracking method may create a need to get away to process what they have so far. There is often no vehicle for easily communicating exactly what is on people's minds, so it is not as obvious to someone of this style when others are not on course.

Potential Pitfalls

In working remotely, it is easy for people of this style to become focused solely on the desired result (as they see it) and for them to not integrate others' needs or goals. They can get caught up in the task and ignore or overlook interpersonal cohesion needs. It is often hard to get to know them well on a personal level when colocated and may be even more difficult when working remotely.

Opportunity for Growth

If this is your style:

- Remember to let others know what plans you have in mind.
- Use the phone to maintain a personal connection.
- Let others know that you are thinking things over and will respond later.

Please Understand Them

The natural independence of this style is not necessarily aloofness. People of this style may be more adaptable than they appear. Their charted course actually may give them more flexibility because they have the time to think about proposed changes.

Support Them

To support people of this style:

- Give them ample time and space to reflect before expecting an answer.
- Show them how the group is on course and the project is moving along.
- Be sure they get agendas and other pertinent data for conference calls ahead of time and a summary afterward.
- Set a norm for conference calls that if someone feels overloaded, a break will be called.
- Use e-mail more often than the phone with them.
- Structure time for everyone to contribute on calls.
- Ask them to share their desired result and the routes they are considering to achieve it.

9

The theme of this style is persuading and involving others. They thrive in facilitator or catalyst roles and aim to inspire others to move to action, facilitating the process. Their focus is on interaction, often with an expressive style. They get things going with upbeat energy, enthusiasm, or excitement, which can be contagious. Exploring options and possibilities, making preparations, discovering new ideas, and sharing insights are all ways they get people moving along. They want decisions to be participative and enthusiastic, with everyone involved and engaged.

Strengths

People of this style will work to get the involvement of everybody. They get others engaged on conference calls, using their facilitative style and enthusiastic voice. They recognize the importance of face-to-face interaction so are likely to be willing to go the extra mile to make it happen. They will let others know what's going on, in their own minds or with the project.

Advantage of Working Remotely

While working remotely does not play to their strengths, it may temper their sometimes too effusive energy and help give space for others to participate.

Challenges for Working Remotely

Working remotely may not provide enough opportunity for involvement to match their style. They may have trouble resisting real-time interactions that are distracting (as when they are remote from their work group but housed with others). Isolation can be a problem for them, so they may not like working alone or at home. They get frustrated when they can't see movement of the group. It is a lot harder to get the embraced results that they prefer since working remotely misses the more emergent consensus that comes from face-to-face dialogue. Even phoneconferencing and videoconferencing often require too much structure to foster this emergent consensus building.

Potential Pitfalls

They may be too busy engaging with some and not respond to others. When the group is not reaching consensus, people of this style may withdraw to seek more positive interactions with others outside the work group. If they don't have a face-to-face opportunity, they might spend too much time on the phone or interacting via e-mail or instant messaging.

Opportunity for Growth

If this is your style:

- Remember to have patience and don't insist on instant replies.
- Do not over interpret the lack of contact.
- Resist the urge to keep the interaction going beyond its usefulness.

Please Understand Them

People of this style need lots of feedback and interaction that their remote environment may not provide. They will want/need time for relationship building. They are at their best in the beginning of a project and may need support and interactive involvement to reach completion. Because they prefer real-time and live interactions, they may leave a task and find someone to interact with. After their initial burst of ideas and activities, working remotely may help them focus.

Support Them

To support people of this style:

- Use phone and conference calls to involve them.
- Use discussion group software for meaningful involvement and e-group discussions.
- Give them lots of feedback.
- Respond to their e-mails as soon as possible, even if it's just to say you received them.
- Provide ways of easily sharing information.
- Call early and often to keep them in the loop during the formation of new ideas. No call is too trivial.

10

The theme of this style is getting the best result possible. People of this style focus on understanding and working with the process to create a positive outcome. They see value in many contributions and consult outside inputs to make an informed decision. They aim to integrate various information sources and accommodate differing points of view. They approach others with a quiet, calm style that may not show their strong convictions. Producing, sustaining, defining, and clarifying are all ways they support a group's process. They typically have more patience than most with the time it takes to gain support through consensus for a project or to refine the result.

Strengths

People of this style have patience for the slower gathering of information and like the opportunity for multiple sources of input without pressure to speak—especially on conference calls, where they are less likely to be judged for not speaking. They naturally tend to do a lot of listening and tend to be adaptable to varying work ethics, cultures, and time zones.

Advantage of Working Remotely

Working remotely provides them time and space for integrating. They are less likely to be misjudged as lacking confidence or leadership. Working remotely almost *requires* leading from "behind the scenes."

Challenges for Working Remotely

When people of this style are working remotely, it is difficult to communicate their open-endedness via e-mail. It is hard to encourage participation of everyone when they cannot encourage it via body language. It is harder to delegate when they don't have a whole picture of someone's capabilities, which people of this style need more than those of other styles. Informal conversations don't occur and their tendency is to not interrupt others when on conference calls.

Potential Pitfalls

They may not get back to each person about what and why they decided on something or how his or her input was included. Deadlines may be troublesome if they don't have enough information and integration time. When they are not actually in a situation, they may ignore things that have not really registered as critical.

Opportunity for Growth

If this is your style:

- Remember that others need progress reports and acknowledgment of requests.
- Let others know you got their e-mail, even if you don't have the answer yet.
- Remember that sometimes it is okay to not have all the time you need.

Please Understand Them

Just because you have not heard from people of this style, don't assume they are not working on something. Their focus on the quality of a product may lead them to not give unfinished, in-process feedback, so it is always good to check in, as they may not think to inform you. Recognize their tendency to overcommit and that you may not know they have overcommitted unless you check with them. They are often surprised when others feel neglected by them.

Support Them

To support people of this style:

- Acknowledge when you use their contributions since their behind-the-scenes work may be even less visible when they work remotely.
- Ask them for help with problems.
- Be sure you give enough space and time to integrate everything.
- Invite their input on conference calls.
- Show appreciation for ways they support you, especially if you have not yet incorporated their input.
- Use technologies that have a virtual whiteboard or another way for them to signal they have input.

11

Things-in-Common

We often relate to more than one interaction style pattern because each pattern has something in common with the others. These things-in-common reveal themselves in the interactions between people, especially in our communications. As you try to sort out which interaction style is the most natural fit for you, you may identify a preference for one or the other of the dynamics that are at play when people interact. These dynamics are

- Directing versus Informing communications—ways we influence others
- Initiating versus Responding roles—ways to define relationships
- Outcome versus Process focus—where we focus our attention when interacting

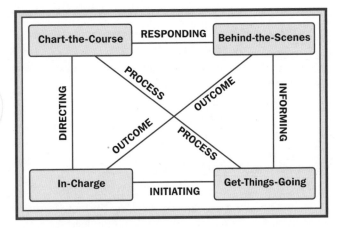

These dynamics are always operating in a situation, and if we become polarized along these dimensions as we interact with others, miscommunication and misunderstanding are probable and likely to result in destructive conflict. However, we need to remember that we always have at least one aspect in common with someone of a different Interaction Style. Draw on these differences when using Interaction Styles to improve your remote working relationships.

Applying Interaction Styles

When working remotely works well, it is often in part because the drives of the Interaction Style are being met, even when the individuals do not know about such differences. Likewise, when it does not work well, it can often be due to Interaction Style influences. An awareness of Interaction Style needs can easily remedy some of the problems.

> *"A leader must spend 70–80 percent of their time tending to remote people for them to perceive he is spending 50 percent."*
> **—Jaclyn Kostner**

> **QUICK LOOK: How working remotely works well**
> Jordan (Behind-the-Scenes) and Sylvia (Chart-the-Course) created many products together using e-mail and the phone, which gave them the reflection time they needed (him to plan and her to integrate)
>
> It worked very well. They often did their "together" work on the phone after hours due to the time zone difference and so they would not be distracted by other work and environmental demands.

> **QUICK LOOK: How working remotely fails**
> Two members of a team were colocated and collaborating quite well. Both had a Behind-the-Scenes Interaction Style.
>
> When they were no longer colocated they became increasingly distant with each other rather than being their former cooperative selves. The sense of separateness was amplified by not recognizing where they had casually achieved synergies when colocated.

How Do You Solve the Issues?

On pages 3 and 4, we highlighted some key issues of working remotely. We have found that a focus in three key areas can make a positive impact on dealing with these challenges of working remotely:

- Building relationships
- Empowering (includes delegating)
- Measuring performance (includes giving feedback)

These are important for leaders or teams who are not remote, but each is more complex when workers are remote than when they are colocated.

These all occur in relation to our different Interaction Styles. As we explore these, let's keep our interaction style influences in mind.

Taking Action

You may wish to make notes from this section on Interaction Styles on the Action Plan on page 29.

12

Building Relationships When Remote

Whether you are a leader, an individual contributor, or a team member, building relationships and trust with those who are remote from you is a key element of working remotely.

What Is "Relationship"?

When asked about relationships in the work environment, most people describe "relationship" as a connection to another. They talk about it as a foundation for working together effectively. The following exercise can help you describe what it is to you.

EXERCISE:
Think of people you have good working relationships with. What behaviors do you tend to see?

When we ask people to share their responses to this exercise, the following are often included:
- Using open communication
- Trusting
- Communicating honestly
- Sharing common interests
- Laughing together
- Building on each other's strengths
- Meeting commitments

Why Are Relationships Important When Working Remotely?

Why is it important to build relationships when you are working remotely? Because people do business with people. And the relationships with those people make the difference in how the work happens. You need to be able to count on people to do their part. It is far easier to count on someone you have a relationship with.

When we are colocated we build relationships informally. We run into people in the hall or at the copier or connect over coffee or lunch. When we are remote, we have to be deliberate about building relationships—we do not have the informal opportunities we have when we are colocated.

What Is Trust in the Work Environment?

A part of relationship building has to do with trust. While we know when trust exists or does not, it is not always easy to define what trust is. We find that in the work environment, trust can be defined as having three key elements:

1. Integrity
We expect people to make and meet commitments. We also expect them to be true to their values. When people don't do these things, we are unlikely to trust them.

2. Competence
In the work environment, we expect people to be competent at their jobs. When we perceive that someone doesn't know how to do a task or job, we no longer count on him or her for doing work.

3. Relationship
As we have discussed, having relationships lets us know others on a more personal level. When it appears that someone is not acting with integrity or competence, we can draw on our relationship and have an open conversation to clear up the situation. Without that relationship we are more likely to assume the other person is wrong or has negative intentions.

What Makes Building Trust Difficult When Working Remotely?

It is generally more difficult to build and maintain trust when working remotely. One key reason is that for many people, trust builds over time. As we have interactions with each other, we have the opportunity to build or break trust. When we are remote we generally interact less frequently. Therefore, it is likely to take longer to build trust.

13

We also find that when we are remote, we don't always tell people when they let us down. Since they don't receive the nonverbal cues to tell them something is wrong, they are likely to continue to work with us as though no problem has occurred. We may feel slighted or hurt and provide no opportunity to clear up the situation. Over time, a few small infractions can become a big issue. When we are colocated, we are more likely to notice the change in a relationship sooner.

Relationships and Interaction Styles

Interaction Style influences relationships from the beginning. We tend to trust those whose energy and presentation of self is like our own. This is the basis of that instant rapport we feel when we meet someone new or even talk to someone over the phone. And early judgments made about the person tend to stay with us in our expectations of what the person will do and how he or she will behave in the future. Each Interaction Style brings a different approach, which will affect the synergies and conflicts in the relationship.

QUICK LOOK: Relationships

Four men joined together to form a startup consulting business. Fred and Jose were located in Seattle, James was in Dallas, and Marco was in San Francisco. The immediate focus of the team was on structuring their offering, building a Web site, and developing prospective clients. They never met face to face as a team—in fact, some of them had never met at all except by telephone. Time and money were both tight, and with excellent electronic tools, they didn't feel a face-to-face meeting was important.

After about six months, they knew they were struggling and got some help. It turned out the four represented all four Interaction Styles. As they interacted with each other they misread each other's intentions, so they lost lots of time and therefore money. By the time they finally focused on building their relationships, too much trust had been lost. It cost them one member of the team.

14

Relationships

Chart-the-Course	Behind-the-Scenes
In a work relationship, people of this style have a tendency to focus first on the task, then on the relationship as they monitor progress toward the goal. Then when they need the relationship to be strong, they may come up short. *Advice:* Remember that it is worth the time it takes to self-disclose and just relate.	In a work relationship, people of this style have a tendency to focus on getting information from one person at a time and thus get buy-in from each person. However, their relationship building may be too subtle, and thus the relationship may not be what they think it is. *Advice:* Remember that it is worth the effort it takes to get back to people about how their input was used.
In-Charge	**Get-Things-Going**
In a work relationship, people of this style have a tendency to focus on the relationship as it relates to the task and therefore more easily get work done through others. Others may feel they don't have enough input to the nature of the relationship. *Advice:* Remember that it is worth the time it takes to give space to others in defining the relationship.	In a work relationship, people of this style have a tendency to need involvement themselves and to want involvement from others. If they get too "hungry" for involvement, they may engage in too many relationship seeking behaviors. *Advice:* Remember that it is worth the effort it takes to make space for others to interact in their own way.

> *"Understanding the diversity of our gifts enables us to begin taking the crucial step of trusting each other."*
> **—Max DePree**

One of the dynamics of Interaction Styles relates to the pace and tone of the interaction. Those with either an In-Charge or Get-Things-Going style have a natural tendency to initiate and use a faster pace in their interactions, while those with either a Chart-the-Course or Behind-the-Scenes style have a tendency to pause before they respond to the interaction. This dynamic gives us clues to the kinds of roles we take with others as well as the kinds of interactions we find most energizing.

Initiating
In-Charge or Get-Things-Going

Those who gravitate toward initiating roles are usually quite comfortable making the first move in a relationship—introducing themselves first or starting a lively conversation. This is often seen as being assertive or one up. People with a preference for initiating tend to be uncomfortable with long periods of silence or in situations that require them to not engage others in interaction.

**Characteristics and Implications
for Working Remotely**

They have a tendency to focus first on what's happening "out there."
  • They may be frustrated since they can't always "see" what's happening with others when not colocated.

They want a lot of interaction.
  • They may be frustrated by not having enough contact with others.
  • They want to know what's happening.
  • Using e-mail can be frustrating when there is no immediate response. Instant messaging can help here.

They initiate interactions with a fast pace.

They are usually expressive in voice tone and gestures.
  • They may tend to dominate and interrupt on conference calls.
  • They may be frustrated by a lack of feedback and engagement.

Responding
Chart-the-Course or Behind-the-Scenes

Those who tend to use responding roles usually prefer to wait for the other person to make the first move, responding to opening comments by engaging in the conversation or giving minimal responses. This is often seen as being reticent or one down. In reality, the perceived hesitance may be a lack of comfort with defining the relationship for the other person. People with a preference for responding tend to be uncomfortable in situations that require them to start a conversation with a stranger.

**Characteristics and Implications
for Working Remotely**

They have a tendency to focus first on their internal response to what's happening "out there."
  • Working remotely may give them less information and role definition to respond to.

They want time to reflect.
  • Working remotely gives them more time and opportunity to reflect.
  • They may be perceived as not seeming to care or not engaged.
  • On conference calls, they may be frustrated by a lack of time to reflect.

They reflect, then respond to interactions with a slower pace.

They are usually fairly quiet in voice tone and gestures.
  • They may not give a lot of verbal feedback on conference calls, so they can be seen as withholding information.
  • They may be frustrated by not being able to give nonverbal cues as to when they want to speak, so they may interrupt harshly.

15

QUICK LOOK: Relationships

A team of four people with three colocated and one remote worked in the same time zone. The remote person felt left out when the colocated people seemed to be sharing information. This is a normal problem for remote teamwork, but it was exacerbated by the remote member having a Get-Things-Going Interaction Style.

He sent e-mails at length, and when there was no immediate response (others needed time to reflect), he felt more isolated.

How Do You Build Relationships and Trust with People Who Are Remote?

There are many ways to build relationships and trust with people who are not colocated. For the ideas below, place a check next to those you would like to try.

One-on-One

☐ **Call for a "virtual cup of coffee."**
Call someone and tell him or her that you are calling for a "virtual cup of coffee." Both parties know that there is no agenda other than to visit. It's as though you walked up to the person in the office and invited him or her to get coffee with you. It's okay to say, "This isn't a good time," and schedule another time to visit.

☐ **Remember special days—service anniversary, birthday, and so on.**
A call or note tells people you know it's a special day.

☐ **When you do come together, focus on relationship building.**
Take time for coffee or a meal. Talk about subjects other than work.

☐ **Track who you've connected with.**
A simple checklist of when you've talked can help you see whom you've missed. If you travel frequently, pull out the list when you have extra airport time and call someone you haven't talked to in a while.

☐ **Send them a certificate for coffee.**
If you were in the same location, you would buy them a cup of coffee occasionally. Send a certificate for a local coffee or juice shop and tell them to have a cup of coffee "on you."

☐ **Ask how they like to communicate—how often, what vehicles.**
Do they prefer e-mail over voice mail? Is weekly communication often enough? Too often?

☐ **Arrange a regular time when you will talk on the phone together.**
Let them set the agenda for this regular meeting.

☐ **Update them on company and department information.**
People need to know how what they are doing is connected to what others are doing.

"Trust is difficult to define, but we know when it's present and when it's not."
—Warren Bennis

> *"Interpersonal dynamics have as much impact, both positive and negative, on the effectiveness of a team as do their technical skills."*
> **—Sylvia Odenwald**

With the Team

❑ **When you do come together, focus on relationship building.**

- ○ Icebreakers can be an effective way for people to connect. See Appendix A for ideas on icebreakers.

- ○ Outings can be fun and provide an informal environment for relationship building. Examples include sports games such as baseball or soccer, bowling, dinner, and so on.

- ○ Rotate locations. Let different team members host meetings.

❑ **Find a common project to work on.**
Working together on something provides an opportunity for relationship and trust building.

❑ **Begin conference calls with relationship building.**

- ○ Use the first ten minutes of the call for each person to share an "attaboy" with another member on the call. This encourages members to think of how other members have been helpful.

- ○ Use the first ten minutes of the call for each person to share one new piece of news.

- ○ Use the first ten minutes of the call for each person to share what he or she is wearing.

❑ **Use collaborative technology to share information and make decisions.**

- ○ Be sure everyone is trained in the technology and the group members have clear ground rules for how they will use it.

- ○ Put pictures of team members in the electronic team space. Scan in photos so all members know what their teammates look like.

- ○ Create a "water cooler" in the electronic team space. This is a place where people can share personal items of interest, such as a new baby, a new car, a vacation, and so on.

❑ **Encourage mentoring.**
People may need help finding the right mentor. Do what you can to help find a partner.

❑ **Ask all team members to take a proactive role in staying connected.**
It's useful to set ground rules for how often people need to check in and on what topics.

17

Does your Interaction Style have anything to do with which of the above tips you prefer?

What would keep you from trying one of the items you did not check?

18

What other action might you take to build your relationships with people who are remote from you?

Taking Action

You may wish to make notes from this section on Building Relationships on the Action Plan on page 30.

Empowering When Remote

Empowering is basically moving responsibility, authority, and ownership for a task or project to someone else.

Who Can Empower Others?

Leaders are clearly in the position to empower others. However, team members may empower others in some situations. For example, when a team member is expected to take on additional responsibilities, it may be another team member who empowers and guides that person as the ownership shifts.

Why Is Empowerment Important When Remote?

When we do not empower someone to take on a task, the implication is that we will stay involved in every decision that needs to be made about the task. When we are remote, the time required to complete the task can often be too long. This is because it takes additional time to locate each other to make decisions that allow the project to move forward.

> **EXERCISE**
> **What's the value of empowering remote employees from the leader's perspective?**
>
>
>
> **Others who have answered this question have said,**
> - "It gets items off my list of things to do."
> - "It develops my employees—so I have more help."
> - "It lets me spend more time on strategic issues."
> - "It is a good retention tool since it boosts people's skills and self-esteem."

> **EXERCISE**
> **What's the value of being empowered from the remote employee's perspective?**
>
>
>
> **Others who have answered this question have said,**
> - "I learn more."
> - "I feel more responsibility."
> - "It builds my self-esteem."
> - "It provides an opportunity for me to grow."

19

Delegating

We find that the inability to successfully delegate sometimes keeps leaders from empowering. Our experience is that we ask employees to do something and give them a due date. We suggest they call if they have any questions. They do not call because they don't want to appear stupid or because they start on the project too close to when it's due. When the due date gets close, we get nervous and we call to check on their progress. This demonstrates a lack of trust and feels like micromanaging to the employees.

Here is a technique that can help the delegator feel more in control, increase the odds of success of the task/project, and provide learning for the employees.

1. Explain the assignment and the due date. Ask the employees to read over the information you give them and agree on a time the next day for them to ask clarifying questions.
2. Answer their questions and set a time and method for them to share their progress.
3. Receive progress information and provide guidance as needed. Set a next progress check if needed.
4. Receive the finished product.
5. Debrief the process. Let the employees speak first about what went well and what they would do differently next time. Add input as needed.

Next time, you may not need as many steps. Over time, you will be able to just give the employees an assignment and know they will get clarification as needed.

Other Techniques for Empowering a Remote Employee

A concern in empowerment is often whether the employees are capable of handling the responsibilities you give them. Providing a mentor to help the employees learn and do key tasks can speed up their ability to take on new tasks.

Training is another key area you may need to consider. If you are not sure of your employees' training needs, do a skills assessment or have a discussion clarifying what training is needed. Then make sure the employees are given time to take the training and the opportunity to apply the learning.

Effective Empowerment and Interaction Styles

Since empowerment involves moving responsibility, authority, and ownership, then individual differences in how we influence others can play an important role in how effective we are when we attempt to communicate in ways that empower others.

All communications that involve getting someone else to do something can be classified as either Directing or Informing. This dynamic involves the style of the communication as well as the words. Those who have either an In-Charge style or a Chart-the-Course style tend to use Directing communications more often than Informing communications. Those with either a Get-Things-Going style or a Behind-the-Scenes style tend to use more Informing communications than Directing ones.

> **QUICK LOOK: Empowering**
> An e-mail fight erupted between two team members. They copied their manager on all of the correspondence. The manager (In-Charge) used a very directing response in her e-mail. She simply typed, "Stop this now," and the fight ceased. She empowered them by being clear and decisive, freeing them up for more productive interactions.

> *"Empowerment is all about letting go so that others can get going."*
> **—Kenneth Blanchard**

Both Directing and Informing communications can fail because they are not specific and detailed. For example, if Linda said to Susan, "Would you please think of an example to put here?", Susan might insert a family example. If Linda had a corporate example in mind, she could have said "Would you please think of a corporate example to put here?" This would be both directing and specific. Likewise, Linda could have been specific in an informing way by saying, "We need a corporate example here." Both of these are more specific than the previous examples. To avoid many misunderstandings of intent, lack of follow-through, frustrations, and disappointment, know when you need to be specific and when you need to be vague.

> **QUICK LOOK: Empowering**
> Zack (Informing style preference) thought he had empowered a team member, Robert (Directing style preference) to write a report by saying, "We need a report on the key learnings from the retreat." Two weeks later, there was no report and it turned out that Robert didn't realize he was supposed to do the task. Jack learned he needed to add a directive to his information, such as, "We need a report on . . . would you (or could you) please get one done by . . . ?"

Language choice is important. "Would you . . . ?" still leaves some choice, "Could you . . . ?" also involves the employee. Omitting *would* or *could* would make the example extremely Directing and would not elicit buy-in and empowerment. However, such direct commands may be appropriate at times.

> *"Giving someone the freedom to take responsibility releases resources that would otherwise remain concealed."*
> **—Jan Carlzon**

Directing
In-Charge or Chart-the-Course

In Directing communications, there is a sense of time urgency to get a task done. The focus is on accomplishment of the task. These kinds of communications are most effective when there is little or no choice about getting certain tasks done or in a crisis. Nonverbal and extraverbal aspects often carry the message of an orientation to "time and task" or getting things done with a sense of time urgency. The intention is to give structure and to direct the actions of others toward accomplishing either an achievable result or a desired result.

Directing communications involve telling, asking, or urging. They may be preceded by an informative explanation, but a direction is clearly given. This direction often has a very definite feel to it, and the passing of responsibility to the receiver is clear.

Informing
Get-Things-Going or Behind-the-Scenes

In Informing communications, there is a desire to motivate people to action by giving information. These communications are most effective when people need to be motivated internally and enrolled in the process so they buy in to the goal or the way things are being done. Nonverbal and extraverbal aspects often carry the message of an orientation to enrolling and engaging others or wanting others to "want to." The intention is to evoke a response or input and inspire others to action toward either a result that is embraced by others or an integrated, best possible result.

Informing communications involve informing, inquiring, explaining, and describing. They are more open, and no directive is given, even nonverbally. These communications have an engaging, flowing feel to them with the option to act left up to the receiver.

Examples
1. "Susan, would you please think of an example to put here?"
2. "Would you please complete this report?"
3. "Linda, please complete this report by 3 p.m. tomorrow."

Examples
1. "I think we need some examples here."
2. "This report needs to be completed."
3. "This report needs to be completed by 3 p.m. tomorrow."

Strengths
- Requirements are less ambiguous.
- Boundaries are clearer.
- Directing communications can provide more security in an uncertain environment.

Strengths
- Engaging and evoking leads to more ownership.
- More options to approaches for implementation are available.
- Informing communications can provide more space for growth and development.

Pitfalls
- You may get only what you ask for specifically.
- Accountability can be shifted without ownership—so the work gets done as long as it's supervised.
- You can get resistance.
- In a remote environment, it feels more controlling. Examples: E-mail often leaves out the nonverbal communications that convey friendliness and liking. Contextual information present when people are colocated is absent, so in remote situations, e-mail may be too brusque or harsh to transfer ownership.

Pitfalls
- People might not know they are expected to do something.
- You may not get the result you want when you want it.
- You can get too much variation in response or "idiosyncratic solutions."
- In a remote environment, you may not be able to see evidence of lack of ownership, so even more may fall through the cracks. Examples: An informing style of e-mail may not request confirmation or give due dates. Contextual information present when people are colocated is absent, so e-mail may be too subtle to really transfer ownership.

Misperceptions (especially in a remote environment)
- People using this style may come off as controlling, too bossy, and always one-up.
- People using this style may seem too definite and not open to input.
- Attempts to empower may feel limiting.

Misperceptions (especially in a remote environment)
- People using this style may come off as manipulative.
- People using this style may seem noncommittal, indecisive, and indefinite.
- Attempts to empower may feel fuzzy and vague and even disempowering.

Steps to Increasing Your Effectiveness in Delegating and Empowering in a Remote Environment

1. Recognize your own tendencies to giving Directing or Informing communications.

- If you have a naturally Directing style (either In-Charge or Chart-the-Course), recognize that even when you give information verbally, it is likely to be perceived as a directive, and when you give directives in e-mail, they will likely sound too harsh and definite. Consider using emoticons in e-mail and instant messaging for feedback.

- If you have a naturally Informing style (either Get-Things-Going or Behind-the-Scenes), recognize that you may not convey the shift in ownership and responsibility you think you do because you do not directly state it, and even when you give directives verbally, you are likely to sound less definite than you think you are being.

- Do not confuse your role with your natural style. Roles like boss, team leader, and supervisor imply a one-up relationship and lead you to think you are being Directing when you are not. Subordinate roles imply a one-down relationship and may lead you to think you are being Informing when you are not.

2. Recognize the styles of others you are communicating with.

- Do not assume their intentions are like yours.

- Do not assume someone's directives are totally nonnegotiable.

- Ask if the sender of the message intends you to take action.

3. Mix your communications. (Yes, this is one time mixed communications work!)

- Firm up Informing communications by asking for a commitment. For example, "Susan, I think we need some more examples here [Informing]. Would you come up with some from your corporate experience [Directing]?"

- Soften Directing communications by giving supporting and engaging communications. For example, "Susan, I'd like to include some more examples and none are coming to me [Informing]. Would you generate some from your working remote experience [Directing]?"

4. Shift your style.

- Match the style of the receiver. If you have a naturally Directing style, use a more tentative tone of voice to invite agreement or buy-in. Make more subtle, open-ended statements of your wishes or desires at times. If you have a naturally Informing style, use a more forceful tone of voice to communicate urgency. Make more straightforward statements to indicate to the other person what to do and when to do it.

- Match the style needed by the situation. When you have a specific outcome in mind and you are definitely delegating, be direct in doing so; otherwise, you will seem manipulative and condescending. When you want to engage the other person's involvement, creativity, and ownership, inform him or her of what you see needs to be done and engage in a dialogue about the task.

5. Watch out for the "whammies"! They will alienate and not truly empower.

- When we are stressed by deadlines, we often use a Directing style—no matter what our natural style is—and the communication comes across more harshly than we intend.

- When we feel put upon and not engaged enough, we often use an Informing style in a manipulative way to try to get what we want.

Taking Action

You may wish to make notes from this section on Empowering on the Action Plan on page 30.

Measuring Performance When Remote

Leaders generally have the responsibility for measuring performance in their organization. Measuring performance has three key elements:

- Setting objectives
- Giving ongoing feedback
- Evaluating

Individual contributors have the responsibility to provide feedback to their manager and to others they work with.

Teams have the responsibility to set team objectives and clarify responsibilities for team members. Teams also have the responsibility to provide feedback to one another. Some teams do a self-evaluation. Others rely on the leader to evaluate them.

> *"Your very best people will respond to what you actually do, what you evidently measure, and what you openly reward—every single time."*
> **—Betsy Sanders**

The Challenges of Working Remotely

When employees are remote, it is easier to avoid spending time discussing performance with them. Performance discussions do not happen informally, so it is critical that time is scheduled for setting objectives, giving feedback, and evaluating overall performance.

How to Set Objectives with a Remote Employee

When expectations are clear, it is easier for employees to perform to those expectations. A method for setting objectives with remote employees is to provide them with a "straw man" of objectives, if needed (or provide them with your objectives so they can write theirs in alignment with yours).

- Schedule time to discuss objectives.
- Listen to employees' suggestions.
- Discuss the suggestions.
- Agree on objectives.
- Document objectives and send the documentation via e-mail.

23

Objectives and Interaction Styles

In any given interaction, we attend to different aspects. Some people are more focused on the outcomes of an interaction. Others are more focused on processes to move things along. The In-Charge style and the Behind-the-Scenes style have in common a focus on the outcome of the interaction or the situation. The Get-Things-Going style and the Chart-the-Course style have in common a focus on processes. These differences are evident in how people with these styles go about setting objectives.

Outcome/Process — Interaction Style Things-in-Common

Outcome
In-Charge or Behind-the-Scenes

With the In-Charge style, the Outcome focus stems from the desire for achieving a result. It helps to have control over the resources of time, tasks, tools, and people to get the result as quickly as possible. In the extreme, people of this style may be quite active in seeking control and may have a tendency to "push things through."

In setting objectives, people of this style are likely to focus more on the "by when" aspect of objective setting. They will welcome articulating objectives and resist too much detail in setting them since they want to get a result quickly rather than taking a lot of time spelling out how that result will look. You can help by thinking of the time frames ahead of time so you have the timeline answers.

With the Behind-the-Scenes style, the best result possible is central so a sort of 'artistic' control is sought over the inputs and the outputs to get that outcome. In the extreme, people of this style may "hold back" until the result is just right or enough input is had.

In setting objectives, people of this style are likely to focus more on the "what" of the objectives. They will welcome the opportunity to define the specifications for the product or the outcome. However, they will resist articulating these specifications without sufficient information and may be more likely to prefer beginning the process without setting objectives because they know the product or outcome will evolve as they begin the work and have more information. You can help by suggesting they find a broad objective that can be fine-tuned as you go.

Process
Get-Things-Going or Chart-the-Course

With the Get-Things-Going style, there is a focus on engaging people in an emerging process, moving things along, and checking in with people along the way. This can be quite an active, energetic process, and in the extreme people of this style may "randomize and scatter."

In setting objectives, they may like to keep things open-ended and general to get the maximum amount of engagement and momentum. They will welcome the opportunity to generate enthusiasm by engaging in dialogue about where the group is going. They are likely to resist taking the time to get detailed and specific. You can help by being sure they are actively engaged in the objective-setting process and by showing your enthusiasm.

With the Chart-the-Course style, the focus is on having a process to follow that will help determine the best actions to take, then monitoring progress along the way. In the extreme, people of this style may stand back and "overplan" without input and become rigid in following the plan.

In setting objectives, they are likely to focus on setting milestones and benchmarks so progress can be measured along the way. They will welcome the specificity that good objectives need and will resist ambiguous and open-ended objectives. You can help by being patient with their detailed process and giving them the time to spell out the details.

How to Give Feedback to a Remote Employee or Team Member

We can give two main types of feedback. One is called reinforcing feedback—where the feedback is designed to reinforce what the person is doing right. The other is called developmental feedback—where the feedback is designed to help the person learn.

EXERCISE
What is the value of reinforcing feedback?

Some common responses:
- It makes clear what behavior works and what performance is considered "good."
- It motivates more of the same behavior.
- It creates enthusiasm.
- It builds confidence and self-esteem.
- It demonstrates involvement and care from the person providing the feedback.
- It makes an employee feel noticed.

EXERCISE
What is the value of developmental feedback?

Some common responses:
- It makes clear that the behavior demonstrated is not appropriate and/or effective.
- It motivates a change in behavior.
- It builds confidence and optimism for future performance.
- It demonstrates care and concern from the person providing the feedback.
- It emphasizes desired performance.

One size does not fit all in giving feedback, particularly when working remotely. Noting the Interaction Style of the receiver will allow you to tailor your approach. If the leader and follower have the same style, the feedback will probably be the right amount with the right approach.

What Are the Keys to Giving Effective Feedback?

Use face-to-face interaction when possible for developmental feedback (or the phone if you have to—do not use e-mail or voice mail.)

- Be specific.

- When giving feedback, change
  - "you" to "I."
  - "should" to "could."
  - "but" to "and."
  - "never" or "always" to "sometimes."

- Use a model that encourages dialogue.

- Use a model for giving reinforcing feedback:
  - State/restate expectations.
  - Share observations.
  - Share impact.
  - Say, "Thank you."

  Example: "Mary, as you know, I was expecting you would complete the project on time. What I observed is that not only did you finish early, you came in under budget. As a result, the customer was extremely happy with the results and would like us to lead another project for him. Thanks for a great job."

- Use a model for giving developmental feedback:
  - State/restate expectations.
  - Share observations.
  - Share consequences.
  - Ask, "What shall we do to fix this?"

  Example: "Fred, as you know, I expect all projects to be completed on time. I see that you finished the Jackson project two weeks late. As a result, we lost the opportunity to bid for the next project. What shall we do to ensure this doesn't happen on your next project?"

25

Feedback and Interaction Styles

In giving and receiving feedback of all kinds, our natural interaction styles can get in the way of giving others the kinds of feedback they want. We tend to give the kind of feedback we want as well as in the style we want it. Others may not feel reinforced for what they are doing well and not encouraged to develop what they need to develop. The good news is that if we know the differences, we can learn to adjust our behaviors to better suit the needs of the other styles.

> **QUICK LOOK: Measuring Performance—Feedback**
>
> Issac, an In-Charge trainer, works in a different geography and time zone than his manager, Leticia (Behind-the-Scenes). Issac became discouraged after delivering multiple trainings—the reinforcing feedback did not come quickly enough and the developmental feedback did not come in time to affect the next workshop.
>
> Leticia did not recognize the problem until Issac was ready to quit. They solved it by scheduling a phone call within one day after each workshop.
>
> The Behind-the-Scenes manager needed to understand that the immediate voice mails that Issac left after workshops had been serving an important feedback function for the In-Charge trainer and were not just covering his bases or self-aggrandizement.

Feedback

Chart-the-Course

Giving Feedback

People of this style do not usually give much feedback. They are likely to focus on meeting or not meeting milestones. They may not give as much positive feedback as some other styles need. Remote situations may feed into these tendencies. They become more focused on the "course" and do not have the casual interactions to trigger feedback responses.

Receiving Feedback

They want their feedback to be quiet, specific, and direct. They want it to be private, given only to them. The remote environment plays to their needs around receiving feedback.

Behind-the-Scenes

Giving Feedback

People of this style may avoid giving developmental feedback since potential bad feelings may keep others from producing the best result possible. It is even easier to avoid in a remote environment. Reinforcing feedback may be more indirect and not recognized by recipients, especially when neither party can see the other's reaction. They may flip to an ungraceful In-Charge style, which feels even harsher in a remote environment.

Receiving Feedback

They like their feedback subtle and gentle with time to integrate it with other information. They may find too much praise almost embarrassing. They want feedback in a friendly, accommodating style. The risk in a remote environment is that nonverbal indicators of friendliness in developmental feedback are missing.

In-Charge

Giving Feedback

For people of this style, the issue is taking the time to give feedback. When in an extreme In-Charge mode, they may skip giving it unless something is interfering with accomplishing tasks. Directness may convey a negative message that they do not intend. They may not recognize the impact of being so direct in a remote environment due to the lack of nonverbal cues to soften the words.

Receiving Feedback

They want their feedback straight and to the point so they can improve and meet others' expectations. They'd like applause and accolades for what is accomplished. In a remote environment, public recognition is less available to them.

Get-Things-Going

Giving Feedback

People of this style are likely to be verbally expressive and not specific. They may focus more on reinforcing feedback rather than developmental feedback out of fear of breaking the involvement. In a remote environment, they miss early nonverbal cues that the person has tuned them out.

Receiving Feedback

They want lots of feedback, especially reinforcing feedback. They like expressive applause and accolades. In working remotely, spontaneous public praise is not easy to do. In developmental feedback, they want the opportunity to express emotions and opinions. In a remote situation, they may miss the interactive opportunities they would have if colocated.

26

How to Evaluate a Remote Employee

Managers of remote people do not see the people working; they only see the work results. In conversations it is important to focus on results.

A caution here is something we call "BLM"— "Be Like Me." Be careful of expecting the employee to be like you.

If you have given feedback regularly over the evaluation period, evaluation is fairly simple. It is nice to do it face to face, but you may need to do it by phone due to distance, budget, and other factors. If the evaluation is going to be negative and a surprise, meet face to face.

> *"What gets rewarded gets repeated."*
> **—Jack Clemmer**

Evaluation and Interaction Styles

It makes sense that there are differences in how people of each Interaction Style prefer to give and receive evaluations. Of course, evaluation is an extension of setting objectives and giving feedback, so those differences will apply here as well.

Interaction Styles—Evaluation

Chart-the-Course

Giving Evaluations
People of this style may want to match the measurement outcome to the objectives and may focus on the path it took to reach them.

Receiving Evaluations
They want to quietly absorb and go away to digest the evaluation; then they may come back with questions and comments.

What to Give Them
Give them time to anticipate the evaluation session as well as an opportunity to go away and later come back to discuss a plan for the next time.

Behind-the-Scenes

Giving Evaluations
People of this style may want to compare the results with a "perfect" outcome that may not have been included in the objectives.

Receiving Evaluations
They want room for discussion about shades of gray, especially after time to reflect.

What to Give Them
Give them time to integrate the evaluation and to discuss in detail what the best result should look like.

In-Charge

Giving Evaluations
People of this style may want to focus mainly on what was achieved or accomplished.

Receiving Evaluations
They want to ask questions and engage in dialogue to be sure they understand.

What to Give Them
Give them control over the resources to make some changes in the future.

Get-Things-Going

Giving Evaluations
People of this style may want to focus more on the person and his or her response than the detail of the results.

Receiving Evaluations
They want to talk matters through to be sure they will be involved in the future.

What to Give Them
Give them a chance to chat about where things are now and how to move forward.

27

Lois (In-Charge located in California) was giving an evaluation to Felix (Chart-the-Course located in Singapore) over the phone due to distance and budget. They connected at 9 P.M. California time—9 A.M. Singapore time. Felix had a conference call with a client scheduled for 10 A.M.

Both Lois and Felix tend to have a time and task focus. Lois delivered the evaluation. Felix didn't agree but didn't say anything. (He needed time to think about it before expressing his concerns, and he needed to anticipate the 10 A.M. conference call.)

The first Lois knew there was a problem was when her manager called to tell her he had received an e-mail from Felix, who was quite concerned about his evaluation.

Lois had taken charge of the relationship and hadn't made space for Felix to relate as he needed.

The insights for Lois were to understand (1) Felix's reflection needs, (2) his tendency to not give feedback, and (3) the tendency of her own In-Charge style to structure the interaction based on her needs.

Their new course for the future is to have regular feedback sessions during the year. At evaluation time, they will have two conversations—one for the evaluation and one for follow-up.

In the remote environment, planning two conversations—one for the evaluation and one for a follow-up conversation—meets the needs of the Chart-the-Course and Behind-the-Scenes styles for reflection. For the In-Charge and Get-Things-Going styles, you may want to set aside more time for the conversation since it is not "just a phone call," and they may have more to talk about than you would have thought.

Taking Action

You may wish to make notes from this section on Measuring Performance on the Action Plan on page 31.

Moving Ahead

Whether you are a remote leader, team member, or individual contributor, you can ease the challenges of working remotely—both for yourself and for others.

First, use your understanding of Interaction Styles to vary the way you interact with your peers, your teammates, and those you lead. Make space for people to work in ways different from the way you work. Have open communications with them about your differences and what works for each of you. When you recognize the differences, you can work together to utilize those differences rather than be frustrated with misunderstandings.

Remember that the Interaction Styles model is only one general explanation of personality differences. Although it is a very powerful and useful model, it does not explain all the differences. Also, remember that people grow and develop, so avoid the stereotyping trap. Interaction Style is not an excuse for behavior. Learn to flex and become more self-aware and you will reap the rewards by becoming more productive as a remote worker.

Second, take the time to build relationships with the people who are remote from you. It is worth the time and money to meet them face to face at least once if at all possible.

Third, empower people who are remote from you. It will relieve your workload and help them grow their skills. Be sure you empower them in a way that is helpful to them and increases the opportunity for success.

Fourth, measure the performance of remote workers. By clarifying their objectives and then giving regular feedback, evaluation will be an easy process.

These key areas are also very important for working with colocated people. What is different when you are remote is that you have to be deliberate about taking action. So, take some time to plan your actions for

- Understanding Interaction Styles
- Building relationships
- Empowering others
- Measuring performance
    - Setting objectives
    - Giving feedback
    - Evaluating

29

Understanding Interaction Styles — Action Plan

To be more effective, I will . . .

Building Relationships — Action Plan

To be more effective, I will . . .

30

Empowering — Action Plan

To be more effective, I will . . .

Setting Objectives
To be more effective, I will . . .

Giving Feedback
To be more effective, I will . . .

Evaluating
To be more effective, I will . . .

Using Your Tools

It is very easy to overuse e-mail and voice mail when you are working remotely. Consider if one-way (e-mail and voice mail) communication can be effective or if you need two-way (voice-to-voice) communication.

Considerations include
- The complexity of the message (sometimes both communication methods are good here)
- The sensitivity of the message
- The need for documenting the message
- The urgency of the message

Sometimes other tools can be useful. Here are some tips on when to use particular tools.

When to Use E-mail

- When several people need the same information
- To create a documented trail of the information
- For nonsensitive and nonconfidential information
- As a supplement to a conversation

When to Use Instant Messaging

- For quick messages/questions
- To determine if it is a good time to talk on the phone

When to Use Voice Mail

- For short messages
- When you want to convey a particular "tone" with your voice

When to Use a Fax

- When a signature is required

When to Use "Snail Mail"

- When you want to personalize a note

When to Use an Individual Phone Call

- When you would like to talk face to face but cannot
- For confidential or sensitive information
- When dialogue/feedback is important to the topic

When to Use a Conference Call

- When multiple people need to be involved in the conversation
- When travel is not practical or is too costly
- When the topic can be handled in two hours or less

When to Use a Videoconference

- When all parties have access to the technology
- When seeing the other parties is important

When to Meet Face to Face

- For large groups
- For starting up a new team
- For very important messages
- When rapid-fire interaction is desired

When to Use Social Networking

- To communicate beyond the boundaries of the team
- For non-confidential and non-sensitive information

Helpful Tips

Here are ideas that you may find helpful as you use a variety of tools in your remote work. When used well, the tools can enhance remote communication. When used poorly, the tools can make a difficult situation worse.

Tips for Using E-mail

- Utilize the subject line.
  - Write a clear subject line so the receiver knows what the message is about.
  - Establish a set of codes to use in the subject line to help people sort what to read now versus later. This is a sample that one team uses. The team members found themselves with short periods of time to respond to e-mail, and this system helped them prioritize. It also helped reduce the total amount of e-mail within the group. The system is this:

    Right after "SUBJECT:" write one of these four codes:
    FYI—For Your Information
      Read when you have time.
    ACT—Action Item.
      There is an action item in this note. (Also put the due date in the subject line.)
    HOT—Urgent
      Read this first. It is extremely important.
    NRR—No Response Required
      Please read now, but if your response is "no," then do not reply—we will assume you have read this and cannot help.

    This may not be the right set of codes for your group, but if you and the group members discuss the needs of the group, you will determine what will work best for you. This system is incredibly helpful in sorting incoming e-mail as well as reducing unneeded replies.

- Keep your e-mails to one page.
- Research shows that most people will not scroll past one page except in rare situations.
- Use 1L on the subject line. "1L" means "one-liner." Follow it with your message—then put nothing in the body.
- Use "carbon copy" judiciously.
- Be very careful about whom you copy and when. An organization that does a high volume of carbon copying is likely to have low trust.

- Write a separate e-mail for each subject. This makes it easier for people to manage and process their e-mail. They can file or delete as they finish with each note. They can also forward a note without having to delete the parts that aren't relevant to the receiver.
- Use the tools of your e-mail system.
- Filters and other e-mail tools allow you to streamline the management of your e-mail.
- Don't use e-mail when talking is more appropriate.
- If you start a conversation with e-mail, once you have replied back and forth three times, pick up the telephone to complete the dialogue.
- Use good writing practices. Start the note by stating what the note is about, then give the meat of the message, then finish with a summary.
- Use attachments appropriately.
  - Some team members may not have high-speed access, and attachments can really slow them down. Be careful that attachments are not too big.
  - When the attachment is very small, consider whether you should just cut and paste the information into the e-mail.
- If your team shares information frequently, consider a shared database for documents.
- Have the team determine the ground rules for e-mail.
  - Agree on how often team members must check for new mail.
  - Agree on the use of any of the above suggestions.

Is e-mail taking over your life?

1. Measure the amount of time you spend a day on e-mail.
2. Determine the amount of time to cut back.
3. Hold yourself to it.
4. Consider writing and reading e-mail only certain times of the day.

Tips for Using Voice Mail

- Identify yourself.
- Leave your phone number at the beginning and end of your message.
- Think through your message before you call.
- State the purpose of your call.
- Speak slowly.

33

Tips for Using Instant Messaging

- Greet the person as you would if you walked up to him or her (e.g., "Hi," "How are you?").
- Use it to let people know you are available.
- After three or four messages back and forth, pick up the telephone and talk.
- Use it for mentoring—your mentee can ask quick questions as needed all day and get your responses quickly.
- Use it while on a conference call to give an individual feedback (in lieu of body language).

Tips for Using Collaborative Software

- Be sure everyone in the group knows how to use the software.
- For shared databases,
    - Agree on how often members are required to check the database.
    - Set up guidelines for where to store information (by project, by topic, etc.)
    - Set up guidelines for how and when to respond.

Tips for Running Effective Conference Calls

- Have a facilitator.
- Take roll so everyone knows who is on the call.
- Be clear on the purpose for meeting (information sharing, decision making, planning, problem solving, team building, feedback/evaluation, training, celebrating).
- Announce people coming and leaving.
- Send the agenda in advance with handouts.
- Start and end on time.
- Watch the clock.
- Consider having someone be a timekeeper.
- Take breaks every one and a half hours, if the call is longer than two hours.
- Follow up the call with brief "minutes" of key decisions made, follow-up items, and so on.
- Use "propose and poll" for decision making. Propose and poll is a process where you share a proposal in exact words. Then via a roll call, each participant says yes or no to the proposal. A no is treated as data and those who said no are asked (after the polling) to share their concerns. After dialogue, a revised proposal is shared and the polling is repeated, starting and ending with different people. It is not uncommon for this process to go on for several iterations.

Tips for Running E-Meetings

- Use the tips suggested for conference calls.
- Use e-meetings for learning or meetings.
- Take advantage of the software's tools for including participants.
- Use e-meetings when a presentation needs to be shown.
- Use e-meetings when the meeting will include creating a document or notes that all members need to see during the meeting.

Tips for Starting Up a Remote Team

When a new remote team is formed, some key issues need to be discussed. The ideal situation is for the team to come together for a face-to-face startup meeting. When that is not possible, you may want to hold one or more telephone conference or videoconference calls.

The following items should all be clarified among team members when starting up a remote team:

- Define the team's purpose.
- Define success criteria and measurement.
- Define the membership (six to seven people maximum is ideal when working remote).
- Define team guidelines/standards:
    - How to communicate
    - How often to communicate
    - How often to meet face to face
    - How work will be assigned and reviewed
- Establish roles and responsibilities. (Consider an e-meeting whiteboard if you are not face to face.)
- Determine how learning and information will be shared within the team.
- Consider how to capture and share with others what the team learns.
- Define guidelines for knowing when the team's work is complete.

34

Tips for Using Relationship Building Techniques

Icebreakers

Icebreakers are useful for relationship building when you have a face-to-face meeting.

Commonalities

Accomplishing work together has to do with more than just doing the task. How people work together affects the quality of what they do. So, building relationships with one another is important.

This activity is a vehicle to help participants build relationships by getting to know each other on a more personal level.

Say, "You have fifteen minutes to find one thing you have in common with each other person here. (Examples: Joe and Suzy both grew up in Oklahoma. Mary and Fred both enjoy reading about and tasting wines.) Once you have found something in common with one person, you cannot reuse that item with someone else."

Award a prize to the pair who have the most unusual or unique thing in common.

Hand out recording sheets. Get people on their feet. Watch the time. Try to provide enough time for everyone to finish. For a large group you may need more time—or you may not have them get to everyone.

Debrief: Have each person share his or her most unusual commonality. Give prizes, if appropriate.

New/Old/Surprise

Give everyone a piece of flip chart paper and markers. Have each person create a chart illustrating "Old," "New," and "Surprise." Everyone should draw pictures showing what is new since the group was last together (New), what is the same (Old), and what is something he or she had not anticipated (Surprise). Then have everyone share. You can post the charts on the wall during your meeting.

Style Tidbits Go-Round

When the team knows the Interaction Styles model, you can open meetings with a Style Tidbits Go-Round. This can be done when on a conference call, over e-mail, or face to face. It gives a structure to personal sharing and helps reinforce the personality diversity concepts the team may have been exposed to. Setting a time limit can help keep things moving.

Each person shares an insight or an example of any of the following:

- How the person's own Interaction Style played out since the group last met
- How a conflict due to Interaction Style differences came up and how the person handled it
- How the person shifted his or her communications
- How the person applied the information in this book

35

People have been working effectively in home offices for years. Yet, not everyone who works at home is as effective as they could be and not all managers feel comfortable managing work-at-home employees. This appendix provides suggestions for both managing and working from home.

Working From Home

Working from home sounds like a wonderful opportunity to most people who commute to work in a regular office. While the rewards of working at home can be great, it is not without its challenges.

Working from home can have some negative aspects that are not always anticipated. Not everyone has a dedicated space in their home where they can work. This can cause many issues like the following:

- Interruptions from family members sharing the space can be a distraction.
- Separating one's business life and personal life can be difficult. Work can be all consuming and can cause stress and family problems.

Another common issue with telecommuting from home is unrealistic expectations from family members. A spouse might expect you to deal with repairmen, household chores, and child care during work time. Children might expect you help with homework and attend after school sporting events. Very young children may not understand that you are not available to them even though you are at home.

Another "not so great" aspect of working from home can be the perception of colleagues who do not work at home. Colleagues or your boss may feel you are not carrying your weight since they cannot see you working. They may imagine that you are doing family or household tasks rather than your work. They may forget to include you in important decisions or to update you on information you need in order to be successful.

The work-at-home world is here to stay, and it works very well for a majority of those who work this way. If working from home is not working well for you, we hope some of our suggestions will help you improve the situation.

Here Are Some Suggestions to Help with the Challenges:

Clarify Family Expectations

When are you "available" and when are you not available? How will they know?

One man we know had small children who did not understand why he was not available all the time. He set up a traffic signal system outside his office door. When the light was green, the children could come into the office freely. When the light was yellow, the children needed to ask permission to enter the office. And when it was red, that meant he could not be interrupted. The system worked great for him and for the kids! You do not have to create anything so elaborate, but you will find it easier to focus if the family knows when they can interrupt you.

Will you answer the home telephone or the doorbell?

Whether you will or will not answer the phone or door is not as important as discussing and agreeing on whether you will or in what circumstances you will. For example, Susan does not answer the home phone or the doorbell unless her husband specifically asks her to. When he is expecting a call or delivery, he lets her know so that she can be alert to that need.

What about laundry, cooking dinner, walking the dog, and other household chores?

This is a continuation of the conversation clarifying that you are working and what that means. If you are self-employed, you may look at this question differently than if you work for an organization.

Interact with Colleagues

Unless the nature of your job has you interacting several times a day with your manager and/or colleagues, you will need to be more deliberate about interacting with them. In the office, they see that you are working and you have many informal interactions during the day. When you are working from home, you are "out of sight and out of mind." If you do not stay connected, you risk missing out on important conversations.

When you do have to go into the office, be sure you take time to interact face-to-face with those people you depend on for your success.

36

Clarify Work Expectations

Every manager is different. Talk with your manager about her expectations for

- Communication
- Results and outcomes
- Availability
- Going ainto the office

Separate Work and Home

Try to create as much separation between work and home as possible so you can put your focus where it is needed. Ways to do this include:

- Have a workspace dedicated to your home office. Only enter that space when you are working.
- Avoid going back into your office after dinner – "to quickly check e-mail." You may find yourself spending all your evening time working.
- Get a business telephone with a ringer that can be turned off when you are not working.
- Create a routine for ending your day. For example, Susan shuts down her computer, turns off her telephone ringer, changes her voice mail message for the next day and empties her trash. This helps her shift gears to focus on her personal life. Another person we know takes a walk around the block at the end of his workday. He finds this a good substitute for the end of day thinking and processing he used to do on his commute home.

Managing People Who Work From Home

Having employees who work at home also has some challenges for the remote worker's manager. Questions and comments we often hear from managers are:

- How do I know he is really working?
- I feel like I am imposing when I call someone who is working at home.
- How do I know my employee is managing all of the potential work-at-home challenges listed above?

Trust is critical when you are managing someone working from home. If you carefully clarify what you expect and have an agreed-to way for you to know progress toward results, you have no need to "check up" on the employee.

If you are managing a work-at-home employee, here are some suggestions.

- Clarify what phone number you are to use when you call him.
- Clarify what results you expect from her.
- Discuss how often and in what situations you need to talk to each other by phone as well as situations that require him to go into the office.
- Determine how you will keep her "in the loop" on issues and changes that will impact her work.
- Agree on how he will keep you informed. This might be a weekly brief status report (results for the week, goals for the next week, areas of concern).

If you are considering having someone work from home, have very frank discussions about expectations. Set it up on a "trial" basis for 60 or 90 days. Evaluate it and determine if it is working for the person as well as for you and the business.

37

Interaction Styles

Alessandra, Tony, and Michael J. O'Connor. *The Platinum Rule: Discover the Four Basic Business Personalities—and How They Can Lead You to Success*. New York: Warner Books, 1996.

Berens, Linda V. *Interpersonal Agility*. Huntington Beach Calif.: Telos Publications, Spring 2010.

Berens, Linda V. *Understanding Yourself and Others®: An Introduction to Interaction Styles 2.0*. Huntington Beach, Calif.: Telos Publications, 2008.

Bolton, Robert, and Dorothy Grover Bolton. *People Styles at Work: Making Bad Relationships Good and Good Relationships Better*. New York: American Management Association, 1996.

Bolton, Robert, and Dorothy Grover Bolton. *Social Style/Management Style: Developing Productive Work Relationships*. New York: American Management Association, 1984.

Geier, John G., and Dorothy E. Downey. *Energetics of Personality*. Minneapolis: Aristos Publishing House, 1989.

Geier, John G., and Dorothy E. Downey. *Personality Analysis*. Minneapolis: Aristos Publishing House, 1989.

Gerke, Susan and Karon West. *Quick Guide to the Interaction Styles and Time Dynamics*. Huntington Beach Calif.: Telos Publications, 2007.

Hunsaker, Phillip L., and Anthony J. Alessandra. *The Art of Managing People*. New York: Simon & Schuster, 1986.

Marston, William Moulton. *Emotions of Normal People* 1928. Reprint, Minneapolis: Persona Press, 1979.

Tannen, Deborah. *You Just Don't Understand*. New York: William Morrow and Company, 1990.

Watzlawick, Paul, Janet Helmick Beaven, and Don D. Jackson. *Pragmatics of Human Communication: A Study of Interactional Patterns, Pathologies, and Paradoxes*. New York: W.W. Norton & Company, 1967.

Remote Leadership/Teamwork

Amigoni, Michael, and Sandra Gurvis. *Managing the Telecommuting Employee*. Avon, Mass: Adams Business, 2009.

Duarte, Deborah L., and Nancy Tennant Snyder. *Mastering Virtual Teams*. San Francisco: Jossey-Bass, Inc., 2001.

Froggatt, Cynthia C. *Work Naked*. San Francisco: Jossey-Bass, 2001.

Hoefling, Trina. *Working Virtually*. Sterling, Va.: Stylus Publishing, LLC, 2001.

Kostner, Jaclyn. *Virtual Leadership*. New York: Warner Books, 1994.

Odenwald, Sylvia B. *Global Solutions for Teams*. Chicago, Irwin Professional Publishing, 1996.

O'Hara-Deveraux, Mary, and Robert Johansen. *Global Work: Bridging Distance, Culture, and Time*. San Francisco: Jossey-Bass, Inc., 1994.

Shipley, David, and Will Schwalbe. *Send*. New York: Alfred A. Knopf, 2007.

Building Relationships

Kaye, Beverly, and Sharon Jordan-Evans. *Love'Em or Lose'Em*. San Francisco: Berrett-Koehler, 1999.

Empowerment

Blanchard, Ken, John P. Carlos and Alan Randolph. *Empowerment Takes More Than a Minute*. San Francisco: Berrett-Koehler, 1996.

Lyles, Dick. *Winning Ways*. New York: G.P. Putnam's Sons, 2000.

Measuring Performance

Blanchard, Ken, and Garry Ridge. *Helping People Win at Work*. Upper Saddle Ridge, NJ: FT Press, 2009.

Buckingham, Marcus, and Curt Coffman. *First, Break All the Rules*. New York: Simon & Schuster, 1999.

Buckingham, Marcus, and Donald Clifton. *Now, Discover Your Strengths*. New York: The Free Press, 1999.

On the Internet

Linda Berens: www.lindaberens.com
Interstrength® Associates: www.interstrength.com
Susan Gerke: www.susangerke.com
Telos Publications: www.telospublications.com

39